GOD'S
ANSWERS
TO OUR
ANXIETIES

GOD'S ANSWERS TO OUR ANXIETIES

JAMES T. JEREMIAH

BAKER BOOK HOUSE
Grand Rapids, Michigan

Scripture quotations designated NASB are from the New American Standard Bible, © The Lockman Foundation 1960, 1962, 1963, 1968, 1971, 1972.

The Scripture quotation designated BV is from the Berkeley Version, copyright © Zondervan Publishing House 1959, 1969.

One Scripture quotation is from the Amplified Version, copyright © Zondervan Publishing House 1965.

To the alumni of Cedarville College
who are engaged in the ministry
of declaring the Savior's
answers to man's anxieties

PREFACE

The world is filled with people who worry. Some are controlled by anxieties about things that never happen. They cross imaginary bridges where there are not even any rivers.

The Bible-believing Christian has a remedy for these anticipated ills. While in prison Paul wrote, "Be careful [anxious] for nothing . . . the peace of God . . . shall keep [guard] your hearts and minds through Christ Jesus" (Phil. 4:6, 7).

The pages that follow present some of our Lord's answers to the anxieties that plague us. The twenty brief chapters are "Campus Challenge" messages which have been presented on several radio stations. It is our prayer that God will use them in printed form as He has been pleased to do by means of radio.

CONTENTS

SIN

Shortly before his death, Robert Frost was interviewed on television by a group of reporters whose questions implied that this was the most difficult time in which man has ever lived. They kept trying to badger the octogenarian poet into saying what they wanted him to say. At last he succeeded in outshouting them and making himself heard: "Yes, yes, it's a terribly difficult time for a man to try to save his soul—about as difficult as it always has been."

It is difficult to say whether Frost understood that it is *impossible* for any of us to save our own souls. With reference to the salvation of the soul, Jesus said, "With men it is impossible, but not with God: for with God all things are possible" (Mark 10:27).

Salvation is humanly impossible because of sin. The Bible says that sin brings death, the unsaved person being ". . . dead in trespasses and sins" (Eph. 2:1). By nature man's heart is ". . . deceitful above all things, and desperately [incurably] wicked . . ." (Jer. 17:9). Man has ". . . sinned, and come short of the glory of God" (Rom. 3:23), and ". . . the wrath of God abideth on him" (John 3:36). Sin has so ruined and depraved man's soul, separated him from God, that his salvation can only be a reality by the power of God.

Because Jesus Christ gave His life on the cross to save us from our sins, the child of God can say with grateful assurance: *1) He bore my sins*—"Who his own self bare our sins in his own body on the tree, that we, being dead to sins, should live unto righteousness: by whose stripes ye were healed" (I Peter 2:24). *2) He suffered for my sins*—"For Christ also hath once suffered for sins, the just for the unjust, that he might bring us to God, being put to death in the flesh, but quickened by the Spirit" (I Peter 3:18). *3) He purged my sins*—"Who being the brightness of his glory, and the express image of his person, and upholding all things by the word of his power, when he had by himself purged our sins, sat down on the right hand of the Majesty on high" (Heb. 1:3). *4) He removed my sins*—"Behold, for peace I had great bitterness: but thou hast in love to my soul delivered it from the pit of corruption: for thou hast cast all my sins behind thy back" (Isa. 38:17).

The great artist Joseph Mallord William Turner once invited a friend to view his latest painting. It was a vivid picture of a storm at sea. After gazing at the painting for several minutes the overwhelmed visitor asked the artist, "How did you ever paint such a realistic scene?"

The artist explained his secret. "I went to the seashore and hired a fishing boat. The pilot took me out into the sea even though we knew a storm was on the way. We sailed into the storm. Oh, how I wanted to hide in safety in the bottom of the boat, but I stayed on the deck, bound to the mast! I did not simply see the storm; I felt it—I breathed it—I lived in it—and I lived through it! Only then could I paint the picture."

As Christ came to this earth and lived among men, He was " . . . touched with the feeling of our infirmities . . . in all points tempted like as we are, yet without sin" (Heb. 4:15). He felt, breathed, and lived through the storm—the storm of God's wrath placed upon Him in our behalf.

Sin, not necessarily personal sins, is the cause of all of our anxieties. Because we are sinners, we have problems. Since Christ died for us, the just for the unjust, and fully paid the sin debt against us, we can claim His victory in our lives. He is the answer to our anxieties.

For further study: Isa. 53:4–7; Rom. 3:10–31; I Cor. 6:9–11; I John 1:8–10.

GUILT

Of all the problems faced by members of the human race, there is none quite so depressing and defeating as that of guilt. Guilt is "the fact of being responsible for an offense or wrong-doing or the remorseful awareness of having done something wrong." Many biblical characters knew the meaning of guilt, and the Word of God repeatedly states in various ways that the solution of this problem has been provided by Christ in His substitutionary death in our behalf.

David is an outstanding illustration of the way a guilty person suffers within the depths of his soul. Psalm 38 records the sorrows of David's guilty heart. "For thine arrows stick fast in me, and thy hand presseth me sore . . . neither is there any rest in my bones because of my sin. For mine iniquities are gone over mine head: as an heavy burden they are too heavy for me. . . . I go mourning all the day long . . . my sorrow is continually before me" (Ps. 38:2–4, 6, 17).

In Psalm 51 we learn the remedy for guilt. Deliverance from this terrible burden comes through confessing the sin that causes the guilt, then turning to and trusting the Savior who has paid the full price of our sins. "Have mercy upon me, O God, according to thy lovingkindness: according unto the multitude of thy tender mercies blot out my transgressions. Wash me thoroughly from mine iniquity, and cleanse me from my sin. For I acknowledge my transgressions: and my sin is ever before me. Against thee, thee only, have I sinned, and done this evil in thy sight. . . . Purge me with hyssop, and I shall be clean: wash me, and I shall be whiter than snow" (Ps. 51:1–7).

All of us are sinners before God, but the sense of guilt can be removed as we recognize that Jesus Christ has paid the debt of our sin by His death in our behalf. Often when we recognize we are sinners and consequently in deep debt, we feel guilty and try by our works to pay the debt and remove the guilty feeling. Good works, at best, only temporarily cover a sense of guilt; they never cure it.

It is said that Henry Clay once owed a debt to a bank that he could not pay. He went to the bank to see what arrangements could be made to meet his obligation. To the cashier he said, "I have come to see about my debt."

The cashier replied, "Mr. Clay, you have no obligation at this bank."

Thinking he had been misunderstood, he said, "I am speaking about the note I owe the bank."

The cashier replied, "Mr. Clay, you don't owe this bank one cent. Some of your friends knew of your obligation and they knew of your inability to meet it, so they made up the sum among themselves and came and paid it. You do not owe this bank a penny."

With tears in his eyes, and unable to say another word, Clay went out to thank his friends for their wonderful display of friendship. Whatever guilt he had because of the unpaid debt vanished when he knew the bill was paid.

We must count our own imagined goodness useless as a means of salvation. We can and must simply accept as a gift what God has done for us through Christ's shed blood on the cross. When you do trust Christ as your Savior, you need no longer be guilty, though your sin may be great. When Christ is your

Savior you can count on God to forgive and forget your sins. He has promised to remember them no more because He has cast them behind His back and buried them in the depths of the sea.

"Being justified freely by his grace through the redemption that is in Christ Jesus: Whom God hath set forth to be a propitiation through faith in his blood, to declare his righteousness for the remission of sins that are past, through the forbearance of God" (Rom. 3:24, 25).

"Who was delivered for our offences, and was raised again for our justification. Therefore being justified by faith, we have peace with God through our Lord Jesus Christ" (Rom. 4:25—5:1).

Whatever your sin, wherever it was committed, and whatever degree of guilt you feel, your guilty standing before God and the guilty feeling in your heart will be removed when you trust Christ as your Savior.

For further study: Isa. 38:17; 43:25; Jer. 31:34; Micah 7:18; Eph. 1:7; Heb. 1:3.

GREED

There was once an unsaved church member of considerable wealth who could never be induced to give anything to any church need or missionary program. On his deathbed he sent for the minister and asked him what he thought would become of him. The minister exhorted him to repent, turn to Christ for salvation, and as a result, renounce the world. The miser gazed at his admonisher in amazement. Give up the world, his treasures—he would not. Even within a few moments of death, under the bedclothes he was grasping the keys to the cabinet which contained his money. He passed into eternity clutching his keys. Such is the power of greed and miserliness as it sometimes develops, leaving God and His love out of life.

In A.D. 79, Pompeii was destroyed when Mt. Vesuvius erupted and covered the city with twenty feet of ashes. In one of the houses of that ruined city the skeleton of a man was found who apparently for the sake of sixty coins, a small plate, and a dish full of silver, had remained in his house until the street was already half filled with volcanic matter. He was found as if in the act of escaping from a window, dead because of his greed.

"If then you have been raised up with Christ, keep seeking the things above, where Christ is, seated at the right hand of God. Set your mind on the things above, not on the things that are on earth. For you have died and your life is hidden with Christ in God" (Col. 3:1–3, NASB).

Greed or covetousness (called idolatry in the Bible) has brought ruin to many. Lot, Balaam, Adam, Saul, the rich young ruler, Ananias and Sapphira are a few of the Bible characters who lost much more than they gained through greed.

C. H. Spurgeon said:

Covetous men must be the sport of Satan, for their grasping avarice neither lets them enjoy life nor escape from the second death. They are held by their own greed as surely as beasts with cords, or fish with nets, or men with chains. They may be likened to those foolish apes which are caught by narrow-necked vessels; into these corn is placed, the creatures thrust in their hands, and when they have filled them they cannot draw out their fists unless they let go the grain; sooner than do this they submit to be captured. How much covetous men are like these beasts.

Grasping for that which they cannot keep, they miss God's eternal blessing which, once ours, we can never lose.

What is God's answer to our anxiety of greed? Listen carefully to His teaching. "Lay not up for yourselves treasures upon the earth, where moth and rust doth corrupt, and where thieves break through and steal. . . . No man can serve two masters: for either he will hate the one, and love the other; or else he will hold to the one, and despise the other. Ye cannot serve God and mammon. Therefore I say unto you, Take no thought for your life, what ye shall eat, or what ye shall drink; nor yet for your body, what ye shall put on. Is not the life more than meat, and the body than raiment? . . . But seek ye first the kingdom of God, and his righteousness; and all these things shall be added unto you" (Matt. 6:19, 24–25, 33).

There are many other Scripture references that deal with this weakness and sin common to man. "A little that a righteous man hath is better than the riches of many wicked" (Ps. 37:16). "Let your conversation be without covetousness; and be content with such things as ye have: for he hath said, I will never leave thee, nor forsake thee" (Heb. 13:5).

Greed for money, possessions, and position has ruined many who have had more concern for greatness in this life than for the glory guaranteed to the child of God in the next.

For further study: Eph. 5:3, 5; II Cor. 9:6–7; Zeph. 1:18; Matt. 13:22; Eccles. 5:10–13; I Tim. 6:5, 9–11.

DEPRESSION

Depression or despondency is one of the most dangerous diseases the world is facing today or has ever faced. Dr. Harold M. Vesatsky, chairman of the Department of Psychiatry at Northwestern University, Chicago, said, "The depression that is now gripping our society, particularly affecting the youth, is growing to epidemic proportions . . . the sense of futility that people feel in the face of war, corruption, pollution, and starvation is a forerunner of lawlessness and depression."

The middle-aged and elderly with a background of life's losses and disappointments are not the only ones who are suffering from this emotional illness. Today young people are the hardest hit with this problem. Some of the evidences of the trouble is an increase in suicides among the young and an addiction to drugs that comes because they want to drown their disappointments. Violence and cruelty, as well as apathy, are also evidences of depression.

Why are people, old and young, depressed? Perhaps one of the reasons, but certainly not the main one, is that so many find themselves incapable of changing the things happening around them. The basic cause of depression is a hopeless outlook on the future. For many, hope for the future was destroyed by their denying the Word of God and turning from the God of the Bible. This trend worsens with each new generation.

Richard L. Evans asks, "Even if the worst were true, even if the end of all things were a certainty, what would we gain by living as if there weren't to be a future? And what could we lose by living as though there weren't? Life without faith in the future would be all but meaningless." Let it be clearly stated, however, that there can be no real faith in the future without confidence in God and His work. He alone guarantees a glorious future to

His people and gives them hope, the cure for depression and despondency.

In that great chapter on the resurrection, Paul reminds us why God's people need never be depressed. "If in this life only we have hope in Christ, we are of all men most miserable. But now is Christ risen from the dead, and become the firstfruits of them that slept" (I Cor. 15:19, 20). Christians are not "miserable" people, because they face a glorious future with confidence. "Blessed is the man that trusteth in the Lord, and whose hope the Lord is" (Jer. 17:7).

An individual's acceptance by God through the completed work of Christ gives the believer glorious hope for the future and a present peace that overcomes the hopelessness of depression. "By whom also we have access by faith into this grace wherein we stand, and rejoice in hope of the glory of God. . . . And hope maketh not ashamed; because the love of God is shed abroad in our hearts by the Holy Ghost which is given unto us" (Rom. 5:2, 5).

Thus, while in a damp, dingy prison Paul could write, "According to my earnest expectation and my hope, that in nothing I shall be ashamed, but that with all boldness, as always, so now also Christ shall be magnified in my body, whether it be by life, or by death" (Phil. 1:20). The hope of the believer then is the "anti-depressant" that helps him face the future, giving him an inner sense of security, and also motivating an outward evidence of godly living. "And every man that hath this hope in him purifieth himself, even as he is pure" (I John 3:3).

None live with more joy and peace than those who rest on God's promises and love rather than on their own fickle feelings. Hope and trust in God cure depression, but a life without faith in God will be troubled with depression.

For further study: Ps. 37:1–8; 42:2–6; 77:7–13; I Peter 1:3–9.

INFERIORITY

It has been said there are three besetting sins that ensnare and defeat individuals who become subject to them—to whine, to pine, and to recline. They are generally committed in this order. Any one of us will terminate his usefulness or "recline" when he begins to "whine" or feel sorry for himself. Inferiority, or a low self-image, can be our ruin. It is true that one ought "not to think of himself more highly than he ought to think," but it is not true that one should think *less* of himself than he ought to think (see Rom. 12:3, 16).

Lloyd Ahelm, in his book, *Do I Have To Be Me?*, illustrates the "whine" to "recline" cycle by the story of a nationally-known boxer who had, in a short time, become the champion of his weight division. Shortly thereafter problems began to develop. He had been a champion so long that he began to dread defeat. Age was slowing him down. He began to consider himself inferior. He avoided his friends and disguised himself so he could go in the streets without being noticed. He became depressed and sour. His wife divorced him. To avoid default of his title, he accepted the challenge of an unlikely winner and lost the fight. From then on he lived with inferiority and loneliness, eventually dying as a pauper.

Several individuals mentioned in the biblical record apparently had the problem of inferiority. God told Moses to lead the children of Israel out of Egypt. Moses' reply was: "Who am I? What shall I say? They will not believe me. I am not eloquent." God's answer was: "I will be with thee. I am the Lord God of your fathers. I will bring you out of affliction into a land flowing with milk and honey. Who hath made man's mouth? have not I the Lord?" (Exod. 3, 4). Elijah faced the prophets of Baal on Mt. Carmel and experienced loneliness and inferiority when he said, "I only remain a prophet of the Lord; but Baal's prophets are four hundred and fifty." God answered by fire, demonstrating that Elijah had a great God to enable him and to answer his specific problems (I Kings 18:22, 38). Jeremiah was called to serve in a difficult time in the life of his country. His answer was, "I cannot speak: for I am a child." God's answer to the prophet's problem was: ". . . be not dismayed at their faces, lest I confound [ruin] thee before them . . . they shall not prevail against thee" (Jer. 1:6, 17, 19).

Although many great leaders of Bible times faced the problem of inferiority as they were challenged by great responsibilities, God reminded them all that He would enable them. No one of God's people is inferior because God is our Creator, Redeemer, and Enablement. An unnamed widow cast all her living into the treasury (Mark 12:41–44). She might have felt inferior because of her poverty, but her heart was right with God, because she had committed her all to Him; there is no evidence of any anxiety on her part. Jesus commended her as the most generous of all who gave their offerings that day. Christians with the problem of inferiority may find the answer to it in Romans 6:11–16, where we are instructed to "reckon" ourselves to be "dead indeed unto sin, but alive unto God." Sin is not to have any reign over His people, including the sin of inferiority.

Bruce Larson tells of a college student who was asked to tell the most meaningful experience of his life. He wrote that, having suffered an inferiority complex all his life, and having been withdrawn and passive, his life had changed because he had his handwriting analyzed and was told he was an extrovert! No Christian needs his handwriting analyzed to discover there are great possibilities in Christ our Savior. No one needs to feel inferior when he is redeemed by the blood of Christ, forgiven of his sins, justified, inseparably related to his heavenly Father, accepted in the beloved, begotten unto a living hope with a reserved inheritance, and given every reason to rejoice with joy unspeakable!

For further study: Matt. 16:26–27; Luke 7:28; Rom. 8:28–39; I Cor. 3:6–9; II Cor. 1:3–5; Eph. 1:3–14; I Peter 1:2–9; I John 1:7–2:2.

FRUSTRATION

This world is filled with mixed-up people battling with their frustrations. They are often so confused they do not know the need of their own souls nor recognize the solution. So many are like the man who said, "It's a shame you had to wake me up and tell me. I'm not ready. I've got to stay here in the weeds and take more rest. I'm not ready for the responsibility."

That was the response of a 51-year-old Los Angeles man when reporters came to tell him that there was a total of $19,219 waiting for him at a Brooklyn law firm. He had been awakened from his sleep and roused from his bed of newspapers under a bridge in the west coast city. "It's nice to lie in the weeds, think and reflect without letting your stomach get boiled up with problems. No, fellows, I can't leave. I'm enjoying life here . . . no worries except where the next bottle's coming from. No taxes, no rush to work or rush home from work." His reasoning makes sense if life is a meaningless treadmill—which it need not be!

Thousands of people are living only for today. Some are poverty-stricken, while others are endowed with wealth; but all of them think that a tomorrow of reckoning will never come. Some, like the reporters who tried to help the wealthy bum under the bridge, must be frustrated with the way certain members of the human family act.

Others are frustrated simply because they refuse or fail to abide by the simple rules that bring peace to the human heart. A card on the wall of a workroom in a southern cotton factory read: "If your threads get tangled, send for the foreman." One day a new worker snarled her skein. Bravely she tried to rectify the matter, but only succeeded in making the matter worse. Finally she sent for the foreman. When he saw the knotted threads, he said, "You have been trying to unravel this yourself, haven't you?"

"Yes," she said.

"But why didn't you send for me according to instructions?"

"I did my best," she said defensively.

"No, you didn't," the foreman replied, "Remember that doing your best is sending for me!" We too have done the best with life's tangled circumstances when we have first called on God to help us. If your life is tangled up or frustrated because you have tried to run it all alone and failed, then turn to the God who specializes in untangling snarled threads.

Often when a person fails, he is tempted to run away and hide. Although he may stay in his hiding place only until he feels that he has the courage to face others, he has really found no answers to his anxiety. The only true cure for frustration is to turn to God in faith and receive Christ as Savior. "He brought me up also out of an horrible pit, out of the miry clay, and set my feet upon a rock, and established my goings" (Ps. 40:2).

"I know that the way of man is not in himself: it is not in man that walketh to direct his steps" (Jer. 10:23). "The steps of a good man are ordered [established] by the Lord: and he delighteth in his way" (Ps. 37:23). "A man's steps are ordered by the Lord; how then can a man understand his way?" (Prov. 20:24, BV). Man must allow God to direct his steps, although man may never completely understand the way. We do our best for the Lord when we recognize Him as Lord of our lives. He has a plan for us and it is our responsibility to find it and fit into it. He will "establish our goings." Then the "tangled strands" of our lack of understanding will eventually be straightened out. Even the sufferings will end in glory.

Faith in God and submission to His will produce patience, the answer to frustration. George Mueller said, "The beginning of anxiety is the end of faith, and the beginning of true faith and trust is the end of anxiety."

For further study: Ps. 73:1–17; Lam. 3:1–26; II Cor. 4:7–18.

INSECURITY

Once a rich king said, "I have now reigned about fifty years in victory or peace, beloved by my subjects, dreaded by my enemies, and respected by my allies. Riches and honors, power and pleasure, have waited on my call, nor does any earthly blessing appear to have been wanting to my felicity. In this situation I have diligently numbered the days of pure and genuine happiness which have fallen to my lot: they amount to fourteen!"

Imagine possessing everything a heart could desire in a lifetime, yet living without security or happiness. This story is duplicated over and over again in our own affluent society. Ask the rich, the educated, the sophisticated, if they have found the meaning of real security, and many of them will answer in the negative. It was Swift who said, "Happiness is the perpetual possession of being well-deceived." That is, the worldly person only thinks he is happy.

One of the great entertainers of the past was a man who called himself the Human Fly. Without the use of ropes or nets, he would climb up the sides of buildings from sidewalk to roof. The performer was climbing up the side of a downtown building one day when the crowd below saw him pause, as if in trouble. Apparently he could not find a place to grip that he might pull himself up to a window ledge. After waiting a few minutes, he apparently found a piece of mortar between two bricks; and using this for his gripping place, he began to climb up. But to the horror of the crowd below, the Human Fly fell backwards from the building and hit the concrete below with a sickening thud. He lay there dead, something tightly gripped in his right hand. When the police opened his hand, they found a handful of dirty cobwebs! What he thought was a sturdy grip turned out to be nothing but cobwebs, and this mistake cost him his life.

Many people are like this today. They trust in religious cobwebs instead of the person of

Jesus Christ. "I do the best I can." "I was baptized when a child!" "I joined the church when I was twelve." "I took catechism classes." "I believe my good deeds will outweigh my sins." Cobwebs do not give one a sense of very much security or hope. One of these days the people with a false security will wake up, but it will be too late.

"That at that time ye were without Christ, being aliens from the commonwealth of Israel, and strangers from the covenants of promise, having no hope, and without God in the world" (Eph. 2:12). "O Lord, the hope of Israel, all that forsake thee shall be ashamed, and they that depart from me shall be written in the earth, because they have forsaken the Lord, the fountain of living waters" (Jer. 17:13).

"That by two immutable things, in which it was impossible for God to lie, we might have a strong consolation, who have fled for refuge to lay hold upon the hope set before us: Which hope we have as an anchor of the soul, both sure and stedfast, and which entereth into that within the veil; Whither the forerunner is for us entered, even Jesus, made an high priest forever after the order of Melchisedec" (Heb. 6:18–20).

"Let your conversation be without covetousness; and be content with such things as ye have: for he hath said, I will never leave thee, nor forsake thee" (Heb. 13:5).

As long as you base your happiness or security on things that happen rather than on the work that Christ has done for you, the peace and assurance you seek will never be found. Riches, honor, power, pleasure, and cobwebs do not afford assurance in time or eternity.

For further study: John 10:27–30; Eph. 2:8–10; Phil. 3:4–9; Titus 3:2–7.

WORRY

John Wesley talked one day with a man who expressed doubt of God's goodness. "I don't know what I shall do with all this worry and trouble," the man said.

At that moment Wesley noticed a cow looking over a stone wall. "Do you know why that cow is looking over that wall?" asked Wesley.

"No," answered his troubled friend.

"I will tell you," was Wesley's reply. "It is because she cannot see through it."

This should remind us that the things that trouble us never trouble God; when we look to the Savior, we will always look over and above our troubles.

When Thomas Carlyle lived in London, his sleep was frequently disturbed by a neighbor's crowing rooster. Carlyle spoke to his neighbor about it, but the neighbor said, "He only crows three or four times during the night."

"That may be," replied Carlyle, "but if you only knew how I suffer waiting for him to crow!"

That may sound ridiculous, but there are many of us who do even worse. We worry about roosters that never crow—things that never happen. Someone has said, "Most things that make us sigh and fret are those that haven't happened yet." Another has suggested that too many people go through life running from something that isn't after them.

A husband died, leaving his wife to raise six children of her own. She adopted twelve others. A reporter came from the local paper to interview her. During the course of the interview the reporter asked the widow how she managed to raise all those children and to do it so gracefully.

"It's very simple," the widow answered. "You see, I'm in a partnership."

"A partnership? I hadn't heard about that. What sort of a partnership?" the reporter asked.

The woman's face broke into a sunny smile as she replied. "One day a long time ago I said to the Lord: 'Lord I'll do the work and you do the worrying,' and I haven't had a worry since."

The Word of God assures us that trusting the Lord is the cure for worry. "Be careful for nothing; but in everything by prayer and supplication with thanksgiving let your requests be made known unto God. And the peace of God, which passeth all understanding, shall keep your hearts and minds through Christ Jesus (Phil. 4:6, 7). "Therefore I say unto you, Take no thought for your life, what ye shall eat, or what ye shall drink; nor yet for your body, what ye shall put on. Is not the life more than meat, and the body than raiment?" (Matt. 6:25). "Cast thy burden upon the Lord, and he shall sustain thee: he shall never suffer the righteous to be moved" (Ps. 55:22).

If you are a Christian and have a tendency to worry, then think some of these Bible promises through to some helpful conclusions. We are told not to be anxious because with thanksgiving we can make our requests known to God. We can then face the problems confidently and know the peace of God. God's peace becomes ours by trusting Him and obeying Him.

The man of the world asks, "Why pray and trust God when you can worry?" The man of God asks, "Why worry when you can trust God and know He answers prayer?"

For further study: Matt. 6:26–34; 10:16–25; Luke 10:38–42; I Peter 5:7–10.

ANGER

"A bad temper runs in our family," is an excuse often expressed by a person with a short fuse. Some people simply do not try to control their angry outbursts because they confess their fathers had bad tempers before them. People make this family trait a warning.

"You have the evenest temperament I ever saw!" remarked one girl to another. "I don't see how you manage it."

"Manage it?" echoed her friend. "I have to! Maybe you don't know that I come from the Black McGreevys? In a little town we used to live in, the children would run indoors when they saw my father coming down the street. My grandfather struck my grandmother, whom he adored, in a wild fit of temper, so that she was a cripple for life. He never smiled again. With a history like that, what could I expect but a life of insane rages? But I wouldn't be like that. I went to Jesus Christ and I said, 'Dear Lord, I know that I can't control my temper. Take control of my life for me.' And he has."

A man attended a civic club meeting where a physician had discussed what tensions and temper could do to the human heart. "I expect to go around smiling the rest of my life," the man reported to his friend.

"Why all the smiles?" he was asked.

"Well, that doctor told us that a temper tantrum—even a slight 'blowing of the top'—had such effect on the heart that it shortened your life by one week. On top of that, it's easier to smile. It takes sixty-six muscles to frown and only twelve to smile. That's a scientific fact."

"A merry heart doeth good like a medicine: but a broken spirit drieth the bones" (Prov. 17:22).

Author Tim La Haye has said, "Anger is one of two universal sins of mankind . . . all emotional tension can be traced to two things: anger or fear." Because of anger great men have suffered great losses. God told

Moses to speak unto the rock and promised that water would come forth to quench the thirst of thirsty Israel as they wandered in the wilderness. With anger because of Israel's murmuring, Moses said to Israel, "Hear now, ye rebels; must we fetch you water out of this rock?" Then, instead of obeying God, he smote the rock. His anger took the place of faith and he was not permitted to enter the land (Num. 20:7–13). Dr. Clarence Macartney said, "More than any other sin, it [anger] blasts the flower of friendship, turns man out of Eden, destroys peace and concord in the home, incites man to crime and violence, and turns love and affection into hatred."

Paul instructed the Ephesians to "let all . . . anger . . . be put away" for it grieves the Holy Spirit (Eph. 4:30–31). We can "put off anger" if we are saved by God's grace and will seek those things which are above and keep our minds on the risen Christ (Col. 3:1–8). God enables His people who are committed to Him to have victory over anger.

Thomas Jefferson said, "When angry, count to ten before you speak; if very angry, one hundred." We must also be very sure that we identify the sin of anger in ourselves and not apply it to others. Someone has said, "That which is a 'nasty temper' in the other person is 'righteousness' in us." The Word of God has a great deal to say about the subject:

45

"Be ye angry, and sin not: let not the sun go down upon your wrath" (Eph. 4:26). "Stand in awe, and sin not: commune with your own heart upon your bed, and be still" (Ps. 4:4). "Cease from anger, and forsake wrath: fret not thyself in any wise to do evil" (Ps. 37:8).

God tells us to quit being angry. This can be done only as we recognize His power and rely upon His promise. He has the power to bring to pass His purposes in His believing people.

For further study: Num. 20:10–13; Prov. 14:17, 29; 15:1, 18; 16:14, 29, 32; 19: 11–12, 19; 25:28; Eccles. 7:9; Matt. 5:22; James 1:19–20.

LONELINESS

Have you ever been lonely? Loneliness is defined as being sad from want of companionship. Several heroes and godly people in Bible times knew what it meant to be lonely.

Elijah, that great and courageous man, felt he was quite alone when facing the forces of evil. He said, "I have been very jealous for the Lord God of hosts . . . and I, even I, only am left; and they seek my life, to take it away" (I Kings 19:14). Later on God reminded him, "I have left me seven thousand in Israel . . . which have not bowed unto Baal . . ." (v. 18).

He really wasn't alone. Though to his credit, we have often wondered why the seven thousand did not stand with him.

There were times in David's life when he experienced the anguish of loneliness. He knew what it meant to be rejected and hated by King Saul. Out of his experiences he wrote, "Make me to hear joy and gladness; that the bones which thou hast broken may rejoice. . . . Cast me not away from thy presence; and take not thy holy spirit from me. Restore unto me the joy of thy salvation; and uphold me with thy free spirit" (Ps. 51:8, 11, 12). In another psalm written by David, we read, "For the Lord loveth judgment, and forsaketh not his saints; they are preserved for ever . . ." (Ps. 37:28). Here we see that David learned the cure for his loneliness.

Though Paul could write that he was "persecuted, but not forsaken . . ." (II Cor. 4:9) and mean it, he was not without his moments of loneliness. As he came to the end of his ministry on earth he said, "For Demas hath forsaken me, having loved this present world. . . . At my first answer no man stood with me, but all men forsook me . . ." (II Tim. 4:10, 16). While Paul was in prison he was aware that his friends outside had turned away from him. Yet he could say that he was not forsaken, because ". . . the Lord stood with me, and strengthened me . . ." (II Tim. 4:17).

There are many causes of loneliness. Perhaps because a Christian has faithfully and courageously been a witness for Christ, he has not only lost old friends, but his opportunity of employment has been terminated. He knows what it means to be lonely. Or perhaps death takes a loved one who has been very close and important in his life. Sorrow brings loneliness. It is even possible to be lonely within a city with thousands of people all around you. Clarence Macartney wrote, "There is the loneliness of the midnight hour, and the loneliness of the desert and the uninhabited isle, and the heavy, depressing solitude of the mountains. But the worst loneliness of all is the loneliness of the crowd—the solitude of the city."

Christians are not immune from this experience of loneliness. However, they are not like many in the world who have no cure for this problem. They have an answer in the Lord Jesus Christ.

First of all, our Savior meets our need with His promise. To His disciples He said, "I will not leave you comfortless [orphans]" (John 14:18a). "We may boldly say, The Lord is my helper, and I will not fear what man shall do unto me" (Heb. 13:6).

Scripture assures us of our Savior's presence. He said, "I will come to you" (John 14:18b). "Let your conversation be without covetousness; and be content with such things as ye have: for he hath said, I will never leave thee, nor forsake thee" (Heb. 13:5).

Few, if any of us, can go through life without at one time or another facing the burden of loneliness. None of us who trust Christ as our Savior need to live with it for long because He has promised to never leave us lonely.

For further study: Deut. 31:6–8; Josh. 1:5, 9; Ps. 46:4–7; Isa. 43:1–5; Nah. 1:7; II Cor. 12:9, 10; II Tim. 4:22.

TRIALS

For every trial God sends, He gives sufficient grace for its endurance. This truth is evident in the lives of many of God's people who have lived in days gone by. Many martyrs have died with sufficient grace to meet the trial of the hour.

When the chain was put about John Huss at the stake, he said with a smiling countenance, "My Lord Jesus Christ was bound with a harder chain than this for my sake, and why then should I be ashamed of this rusty one?"

When the fagots were piled up to Huss's neck, the Duke of Bavaria tried to get Huss to recant his belief in the Word. But Huss said, "No, I never preached any doctrine of an evil tendency, and what I taught with my lips I now seal with my blood." Huss then said to the executioner, "You are now going to burn a goose (Huss signifying 'goose' in the Bohemian language), but in a century you will have a swan whom you can neither roast nor boil." True prophecy! Martin Luther came about a hundred years after and he had a swan for his coat of arms.

This testimony should encourage everyone who is facing trials today. God knows the testing we face and will not permit us to suffer more than we can endure by His grace. "There hath no temptation taken you but such as is common to man: but God is faithful, who will not suffer you to be tempted above that ye are able; but will with the temptation also make a way to escape, that ye may be able to bear it" (I Cor. 10:13). Someone has said, "Sometimes God calms the storm. Sometimes He permits the storm to rage, but calms His child."

"My brethren, count it all joy when ye fall into divers temptations; Knowing this, that the trying of your faith worketh patience. . . . Blessed is the man that endureth temptation: for when he is tried, he shall receive the crown of life, which the Lord hath promised to them that love him." (James 1:2, 3, 12).

One night on the wild Newfoundland coast, a fierce storm arose before the fishing fleet could reach the harbor. Wives and children strained their tear-dimmed eyes hoping to see the coming sails through the darkness and tempest. About midnight it was discovered that the cottage of one of the fishermen was on fire, and notwithstanding all their efforts, it was destroyed. When morning dawned the fleet was found safely anchored in the bay. As the wife went to greet her husband with the tidings of her loss, he said: "I thank God for the burning house, for it was by its light that the fleet was able to make it to port; but for the fire we had all perished."

"But the Lord is faithful, who shall stablish you, and keep you from evil (II Thess. 3:3). "For in that he himself hath suffered being tempted, he is able to succor them that are tempted" (Heb. 2:18).

"Because thou hast kept the word of my patience, I also will keep thee from the hour of temptation, which shall come upon all the world, to try them that dwell upon the earth" (Rev. 3:10).

George Mueller was once asked how men could develop strong faith. "The only way," replied the patriarch of faith, "to learn strong faith is to endure great trials. I have learned my faith by standing firm amid severe testings." This is very true. It is always time to trust before enduring trials. From the spiritual point of view, they are necessary. We can be used of God only as we experience suffering so that He can comfort and show us how great He is.

For further study: Ps. 44:15–17; 119:49–56, 81–88, 157, 161; Dan. 3:16–18; Luke 6:22–23; John 12:23–26; 16:33; Heb. 10:32–34; I Peter 4:12–19.

FEAR

Fear is one of man's greatest adversaries. An ancient legend illustrates the point. According to the story, a man was driving to Constantinople. He was stopped by an old woman who asked him for a ride. As they journeyed toward the city he looked at her and became frightened and asked who she was. She replied, "I am Cholera."

When he heard that word he was more frightened than ever and ordered her to leave his wagon and walk. She promised him she would not kill more than five people in Constantinople. She handed him a dagger and said it was the only weapon that could kill her. Then she said, "I shall meet you in two days. If I break my promise, you may stab me."

Within two days one hundred twenty people died in Constantinople. The enraged man found the woman called "Cholera" and raised the dagger to kill her. She stopped him, saying, "I have kept my agreement. I killed only five. Fear killed the others."

Some of the greatest heartaches known to man come from the fear of trouble rather than from trouble itself. Too many spend time crossing bridges where no rivers even exist. Clarence Macartney said, "Fear betrays man's spirit, breaks down his defense, disarms him in the battle, unfits him for the work of life, and adds terror to the dying bed." God has a cure for our fears. "The fear of man bringeth a snare: but whoso putteth his trust in the Lord shall be safe" (Prov. 29:25).

During the last war a four-year-old child was among the refugees that came to the United States. His parents had been killed in the raids on Rotterdam. He was filled with fear. Strange noises made him cringe. When he heard an airliner overhead he would run for the cellar. Gradually through kindness and patience, his foster parents taught him not to run away *from* what caused him fear, but to run *to* his new parents instead. In their friendly arms he soon learned not to be afraid. That is the lesson God would teach His children—not to run *from* what frightens them—but to run *to* His arms where they will find protection and comfort.

One of the ways to counter fear in the heart is to consider the "fear nots" in the Bible. "Say to them that are of a fearful heart, Be strong, *fear not:* behold, your God will come with vengeance, even God with a recompence; he will come and save you" (Isa. 35:4; italics here and in following verses are mine).

"Fear not: for I am with thee: I will bring thy seed from the east, and gather thee from the west" (Isa. 43:5).

"And *fear not* them which kill the body, but are not able to kill the soul: but rather fear him which is able to destroy both soul and body in hell" (Matt. 10:28).

"Are not two sparrows sold for a farthing? and one of them shall not fall on the ground without your Father. But the very hairs of your head are all numbered. Fear ye not therefore, ye are of more value than many sparrows" (Matt. 10:29-31).

"And when I saw him, I fell at his feet as dead. And he laid his right hand upon me, saying unto me, *Fear not;* I am the first and the last" (Rev. 1:17).

The living Christ becoming the personal Savior of a person gripped with fear brings peace for the present and hope for the future.

For further study: Ps. 49:5; Isa. 35:3; Matt. 10:24–31; Acts 27:23–25.

AGING

Scientists have been working on methods to keep us all from aging. As time goes on we are supposed to have longer life spans—if the scientific formulas really work. Here is one proposed solution for wrinkles. After hearing about the remedy, you may prefer the signs of aging instead.

Wrinkles can be postponed, it is said, by a simple secret. Make a tepid bath in which you stir bran. Follow by long friction, until the flesh fairly shines. Next, smooth out lines in the face and forehead with unsalted butter.

Finally, mix a cup of oatmeal with cold water into a rather thick paste. Spread this over the face and knead it until it falls off by itself, as it will, in flakes. At this point you will find yourself not only smooth-skinned, but sitting in a bathtub full of warm bran, butter, and oatmeal flakes. Now pour sugar and Half-and-Half over your knees and you will have an exceptionally nutritious breakfast—which is more than you can say for some other modern beauty aids. This solution for the marks of old age is as good as any other for the simple reason that no one can remove the wrinkles nor stop the clock's aging process.

"The days of our years are threescore years and ten; and if by reason of strength they be fourscore years, yet is their strength labour and sorrow; for it is soon cut off, and we fly away" (Ps. 90:10).

Sometimes older people, in troubled isolation, grow despondent: "I guess we are just sitting here waiting to die. . . . When I die, I'll be back with my people again. . . . I have lived too long. . . . No one needs me, and I don't either." We are told that in 1900 there were an estimated 3,300,000 people over age sixty-five in the United States. Each day 4,000 Americans celebrate their sixty-fifth birthday. By the year 2000 there will be an estimated 33,000,000 Americans age sixty-five and older.

We can be sure of the presence and blessings of God upon our lives when old age comes because our God does not change with time. Spiritually, elderly and teenage believers have the same promises in common. Everyone who is born again may claim God's promise for:

1. *The assurance of salvation.* "Verily, verily, I say unto you, He that heareth my word, and believeth on him that sent me, hath everlasting life, and shall not come into condemnation; but is passed from death unto life" (John 5:24).

2. *The presence of the Holy Spirit.* "And I will pray the Father, and he shall give you another Comforter, that he may abide with you forever; even the Spirit of truth; whom the world cannot receive, because it seeth him not, neither knoweth him: but ye know him; for he dwelleth with you, and shall be in you" (John 14:16, 17).

3. *The promise of an eternal inheritance.* "Blessed be the God and Father of our Lord Jesus Christ, which according to his abundant mercy hath begotten us again unto a lively hope by the resurrection of Jesus Christ from the dead, To an inheritance incorruptible, and undefiled, and that fadeth not away, reserved in heaven for you, Who are kept by the power of God through faith unto salvation ready to be revealed in the last time" (I Peter 1:3-5).

4. *The guarantee of a new body.* "Behold, I shew you a mystery; We shall not all sleep,

but we shall all be changed, In a moment, in the twinkling of an eye, at the last trump: for the trumpet shall sound, and the dead shall be raised incorruptible, and we shall be changed" (I Cor. 15:51–52).

Every believer, regardless of his age, has Christ in him, the hope of glory. One day very soon every Christian, old and young alike, will have a new body without spot or wrinkle.

For further study: Ps. 37:25–29; 90:1–4; 92:13, 14; Eccles. 6:3, 6; Isa. 46:4; Titus 2:2–6.

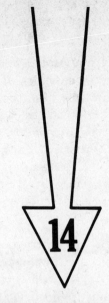

BITTERNESS

The story is told of a servant who had been solemnly warned by his master to stay away from a certain cave. The master told him, "If you even go near that cave, a fierce beast will spring forth and devour you." The servant did not believe him. He had never seen such an animal and supposed that it did not even exist. He even imagined that his master had some treasure stored in that cave and had given him the warning only to deceive him. One day he found the courage to enter the cave. As he passed through the entrance, a great beast leaped from the shadows and devoured him.

God has given us some solemn warnings about sin and its consequences in His Word. Sometimes those who have been warned, yet disobey, become bitter. Instead of being literally devoured by a wild beast they are devoured by bitterness that lingers long in the soul. Anyone who knows what sin will do, yet disobeys, has no right to be bitter about the consequences—but thousands of people are bitter, anyway.

Ralph Barton, the internationally known cartoonist whose drawings appeared in *Life, Puck,* and *Liberty,* as well as in other noted publications, committed suicide at the age of forty. In addition to the pathetic farewell note which he wrote, he penned the following lines describing so graphically the bitterness of sin:

> "I have had my will, tasted every pleasure; I have drunk my fill of the purple measure. It has lost its zest; sorrow is my guest; Oh, the lees are bitter, bitter—give me rest. Love once filled my bowl, running over with blisses; made my very soul drunk with crimson kisses. But I drank it dry; love had passed me by, oh, the lees are bitter, bitter—let me die."

The poet, Paul Lawrence Dunbar, a native of Dayton, Ohio, described the surprise of sin's bitterness:

"This is the price I pay just for one riotous day. Years of regret and of grief and sorrow without relief. Suffer it I will, my friend, suffer it until the end, until the grave shall give relief. Small was the thing I bought, small was the thing at best, small was the debt, I thought, but, O God!!—the interest."

In spite of our weakness, disobedience, and the results that accrue because of them, God has a remedy for a bitter attitude. It begins with confession of sin and a return to Him in faith and repentance.

"What shall I say? he hath both spoken unto me, and himself hath done it: I shall go softly all my years in the bitterness of my soul. . . . Behold, for peace I had great bitterness: but thou hast in love to my soul delivered it from the pit of corruption: for thou hast cast all my sins behind thy back" (Isa. 38:15, 17).

"He hath filled me with bitterness, he hath made me drunken with wormwood. . . . And I said, My strength and my hope is perished from the Lord. . . . It is of the Lord's mercies that we are not consumed, because his compassions fail not. They are new every morning: great is thy faithfulness" (Lam. 3:15, 18, 22–23).

"Let all bitterness, and wrath, and anger, and clamour, and evil speaking, be put away from you, with all malice: And be ye kind one to another, tenderhearted, forgiving one another, even as God for Christ's sake hath forgiven you" (Eph. 4:31–32). A bitter attitude never wins a spiritual battle nor makes a happy Christian. Christians, those who have been born from above, have no reason to be bitter because they are citizens of heaven.

For further study: Ruth 1:19–21; Lam. 3:19–20; Job 9:16–20; Ps. 60, 64; Isa. 51:17–23; Col. 3:8, 19; James 3:14–15.

DOUBT

When a certain teenager was presented with the message of the gospel and the authority of the Scriptures, he looked at the Christian worker with disgust and said, "Look, I'm taught five days a week to believe nothing." He was one of many who believe that it is fashionable to doubt everything that comes his way. Some young people believe it is old-fashioned to believe anything. Sometimes their views of doubt are adopted because of the pressure of friends and their theories. This cult of doubt has some of its foundation in the anti-Christian philosophies that have been and are still being taught in many of our high schools and colleges.

Well-known German philosopher Friedrich Wilhelm Nietzsche wrote, "There are no eternal facts, as there are no absolute truths." Since the Word of God teaches absolute truth, Nietzsche's statement is in direct conflict with it. Since it is fashionable to doubt, young people who want to be popular in the so-called intellectual realm join the cult of the doubters.

Unbelief and doubt may at first sound intellectually attractive, but the Bible teaches and experience demonstrates that life without Jesus Christ's eternal and absolute truths and standards is really not life as God intended it to be. In fact, ". . . he that hath not the Son of God hath not life" (I John 5:12).

When we think of doubters, we generally turn to John 20 and read about Thomas, one of the Lord's disciples. When he was told of the resurrection of Christ he said, "Except I shall see . . . I will not believe (v. 25). If we can discover why Thomas doubted, we may be able to understand why some are members of the doubters' cult today.

To begin with, Thomas would not accept the testimony of others who had seen the resurrected Christ. They said, "We have seen the Lord." The present generation has been taught to question everything and doubt everyone. It is common for many to reply as did Thomas, "I will not believe." In New Testament times, as now, there have been many whose lives have been transformed by a personal experience with Christ. They tell the truth when they say, "We have seen the Lord."

In reality Thomas, like so many of his modern-day friends, doubted because he was ignorant. When Jesus appeared to his disciples, "Thomas . . . was not with them" (v. 24). For whatever reason, Thomas did not avail himself of the evidence that was at his disposal. Most people who doubt God's Word today are actually ignorant of what it says or means.

Instead of believing what Christ had said about His death and resurrection, often predicted before He went to the cross, Thomas was putting his confidence in his feelings or senses. "Except I shall see . . . and put my finger into the print of the nails . . . I will not believe." In this day of experience theology, too many put more confidence in what they can see, feel, or otherwise experience than they do in what God has said. They doubt God's truth and believe their experience which may be contrary to what God says.

What is our Lord's answer to doubt? Jesus said, ". . . Peace be unto you. Then saith he to Thomas, Reach here thy finger, and behold my hands . . . be not faithless but believing"

(John 20:26, 27). Christ made the evidence available, but Thomas had to believe His Word to make it personal. The cure for doubt then and now is taking God at His Word. "So then faith cometh by hearing, and hearing by the word of God" (Rom. 10:17).

Though you may live in a doubting age and find yourself daily surrounded by those who ridicule the Word of God, you may avail yourself of God's protecting armor by reading and studying God's Word. When you are tempted to doubt, turn to His promises and triumph.

For further study: Ps. 42:5, 6; Matt. 14:29–31; John 14:8–11; 20:24–31.

DEATH

Westminster Abbey in London contains the bodies of many of England's heroes. Some were great in the realm of politics, others in religion; others were poets or military men or were distinguished in other ways. Many were good men and some were probably bad, but all of them are dead. The Abbey is a great monument to the frailty of human life. It reminds us that human leadership lasts but for a brief time. The days of a man are threescore years and ten, but he is "soon cut off." Death is an inescapable reality.

Hubert Eaton became a millionaire by softening the harshness of death for relatives of those buried in Forest Lawn Memorial Park in Glendale, California. Here the crumbling bodies of many movie stars and other famous people lie surrounded by rolling lawns, sparkling fountains, and marble statuaries. Eaton said he wanted to "erase all signs of mourning." Death became "leave-taking"; a corpse became "the loved one" who was treated by skilled cosmetologists in a luxuriously furnished "slumber room."

Eaton died at age eighty-five and his own funeral was one to remember. He lay in state in the Memorial Court of Honor. Special music was delivered by the famed Roger Wagner Chorale. Tenor Brian Sullivan sang the hymn "Softly and Tenderly." Governor Goodwin Knight delivered a "narration." Then as the organ thundered "The Battle Hymn of the Republic," the lavish casket was placed alongside his wife in "The Westminster Hall of America."

None of this ceremony cancels the reality of death. Behind the disguised words, the costly cosmetology, and the beautiful music, lies the mark of the great conqueror. Man has no power of himself to cancel the harsh reality of death.

Death is an enemy. It is the last one to be conquered, but it will be defeated. For the Christian there is victory now as he faces the experience that takes him from time to eternity. There are many testimonies relating how God's people have encountered death with victory. R. F. Horton relates that Fanny Crosby in her last illness remarked, "How can anyone call it a dark valley? It is all light and love!" Then stretching her arms out to Christ, she whispered, "I could run to meet Him."

When Dwight L. Moody became ill he was rushed home to Massachusetts where in his last moments he said to his son, "This is no dream, Will. If this be death, it is inexpressibly sweet. Earth is receding, heaven is opening, God is calling, and I must go."

Paul wrote, "For me to live is Christ, and to die is gain" (Phil. 1:21). He further suggests that if the decision to die and be with Christ or remain in this world were his alone, he would ". . . desire to depart, and to be with Christ; which is far better" (Phil. 1:23). He could say this, because living for Christ was his great goal in life.

The word "depart" refers to loosening the moorings in preparation to set sail and is used in other writings to describe a boat leaving port. Death for the Christian is a departure from this earth which instantaneously brings us to heaven with Christ. At the end of his journey Paul testified, "I am now ready to be offered, and the time of my departure is at hand" (II Tim. 4:6). A Christian will not consider death as a penalty for sin. For him it is only a process of change. At death he exchanges earth for heaven.

If you cannot say, "For to me to live is Christ," you can never say, "to die is gain." Under these circumstances you live only to die and that with great loss.

For further study: Ps. 31:5; 116:15; I Thess. 4:13–18; II Tim. 4:6–8; Rev. 14:13.

ILLNESS

Few of us will live our lives without eventually becoming ill. Some will experience tragedy, face extreme pain, and suffer for many years. Many of those who suffer may be tempted to ask, "Why?" E. F. Gallahue in his book, *Edward's Odyssey,* said: "It is easier to explain the who, what, when, and where of a tragedy than it is the why. Human suffering is one of life's greatest puzzles. Why does God allow an earthquake to snuff out the lives of thousands of persons? Why does He allow a drunken driver to kill an innocent child? Why is a teenager struck with lifelong paralysis? Why are some children born into homes of squalor and crime where they never have a chance? Why do many persons suffer agonizing pain for months or years before death releases them?

For Christians no illness or suffering will be eternal. "For I reckon that the sufferings of this present time are not worthy to be compared with the glory which shall be revealed to us" (Rom. 8:18).

Should patients be told about the seriousness of their illness? Will this information increase the worry and produce another "Why me?" Will some kinds of treatment offered by physicians encourage the patients to refuse treatment, causing them to suffer as well as to question? Here is one answer to the question suggested by Dr. Paul Young who, with his associate Dr. Thomas Rardin, conducted a study on this subject in Asheville, North Carolina. He said many of his patients became fearful about the side effects, such as eye damage, of some of the new drugs used in treating arthritis. As a result, many patients failed to show up for periodic precautionary eye exams. To combat this fear, the physicians began handing out a simply worded instruction sheet explaining the treatment and the drugs' various side effects. The instruction sheet "worked marvels," said Young. "Apprehension of patients about eye tests decreased to almost zero and patient cooperation greatly increased." Young contends that physicians should tell patients the whole truth about the seriousness of their medical problems.

The "why" is never answered, the fear is never removed, the disease is never cured, nor the pain ever removed by avoiding reality. Most of the time most people, Bible-believing Christians especially, should know the truth about their illness. The Bible-believing Christian has a Physician who majors in healing broken hearts and mending twisted hopes.

"He healeth the broken in heart, and bindeth up their wounds" (Ps. 147:3). "The spirit of the Lord God is upon me; because the Lord hath anointed me to preach good tidings unto the meek; he hath sent me to bind up the brokenhearted, to proclaim liberty to the captives, and the opening of the prison to them that are bound; To proclaim the acceptable year of the Lord, and the day of vengeance of our God; to comfort all that mourn" (Isa. 61:1–2). "But unto you that fear my name shall the Sun of righteousness arise with healing in his wings" (Mal. 4:2a). "Bless the Lord, O my soul, and forget not all his benefits: who forgiveth all thine iniquities; who healeth all thy diseases" (Ps. 103:2–3). "Call unto me, and I will answer thee, and shew thee great and mighty things, which thou knowest not" (Jer. 33:3).

We have a God who in His sovereign plan can and often does heal the sick. When He does not heal He can and will enable His people to suffer sickness and pain for His glory. Therefore, an ill Christian has a good reason to know the truth about his condition.

For further study: Job 5:6–11; Ps. 17:5–6; 37:23–24; 66:10–12; 119:50, 67, 71, 92, 143; 140:12; Isa. 43:2; Matt. 10:29–31; John 14:1, 18, 27; Rom. 5:3–4; II Cor. 4:17; Heb. 4:15–16.

DISCOURAGEMENT

English clergyman, Leslie D. Weatherhead, watched a group of Persian weavers making beautiful carpets. Their fingers moved deftly under the directions of a master artist who had designed the pattern and who was responsible for seeing that it was executed faithfully. Weatherhead asked what happened if a weaver should make a mistake, use the wrong stroke of the shuttle, or get his colors mixed. The artist announced that usually the weaver does not have to take out the wrong pattern or color. He simply weaves the mistake into his pattern. God often cures discouragement by showing us He has worked it all into His plan for us. "The steps of a good man are ordered by the Lord: and he delighteth in his way. Though he fall, he shall not be utterly cast down: for the Lord upholdeth him with his hand" (Ps. 37:23–24).

G. A. Young returned to what had been his home to find it in ashes. Here and there the smoke was curling up around some indestructible remnant. As Mr. Young stood there his heart was sad, but he found deep consolation in remembering the priceless things he possessed which could not be destroyed by fire. Thus his mind formed the lines: "Some through the waters, some through the flood. Some through the fire, but all through the blood."

The song soon became popular in a small way, but it required nearly thirty years to bring it to the attention of Christian people everywhere. As far as it is known, this is the only song written by G. A. Young. What encouragement it gives to the discouraged soul!

God does not intend that we should be conquered by or consumed in our trials and discouragements. "When thou passest *through* the waters, I will be with thee; and *through* the rivers, they shall not overflow thee: when thou walkest *through* the fire, thou shalt not be burned; neither shall the flame kindle upon thee" (Isa. 43:2; italics mine).

Satan is an enemy always seeking our defeat. When he succeeds, we can become discouraged. Discouraged Christians never win battles or accomplish much for God. This is why discouragement is one of the devil's most useful tools. On the other hand, Christ is our Savior and has made victory a constant reality. He is the cure for spiritual defeat and the secret of an encouraging Christian experience. "Fear thou not; for I am with thee: be not dismayed; for I am thy God: *I will strengthen thee;* yea, *I will help thee;* yea, *I will uphold thee* with the right hand of my righteousness. For I the Lord thy God will hold thy right hand, saying unto thee, Fear not; *I will help thee.* When the poor and needy seek water, and there is none, and their tongue faileth for thirst, I the Lord will hear them, *I* the God of Israel *will not forsake them"* (Isa. 41:10, 13, 17; italics mine).

The discouragements that come our way, though great, are not insurmountable because nothing touches God's people before it has reached His Son, and Christ the Savior lives as victor over all of them. For that reason the apostle John could write, "For whatsoever is born of God *overcometh the world:* and this is the victory that *overcometh the world,* even our faith. Who is he that *overcometh the world,* but he that believeth that Jesus is the Son of God?" (I John 5:4–5; italics mine). "Ye are of God, little children, and have over-

81

come them: because greater is he that is in you, than he that is in the world. Whosoever shall confess that Jesus is the Son of God, God dwelleth in him, and he in God" (I John 4:4, 15).

Discouraged Christians see their disappointments close at hand with God far away in the distance. Discouragement disappears when we know He is near to help us in the time of trouble.

For further study: Ps. 31:22; Prov. 13:12; Isa. 50:4–10; Mic. 7:1–7; Matt. 10:29–31; John 16:20–22, 33.

CRITICISM

The fierce-tempered American short-story writer Ambrose Bierce severely criticized American poet James Whitcomb Riley. When asked how he responded to the criticism, Riley said, "I hit him with a chunk of silence."

Abraham Lincoln declared that if he read all the criticisms directed at him, he would have had time for nothing else.

Lord Byron wrote, "As soon seek roses in December, ice in June; hope constancy in wind, or corn in chaff; believe a woman or an epitaph or any other thing that's false, before you trust in critics."

And the apostle Paul said, "Now I beseech you, brethren, mark them which cause divisions and offences contrary to the doctrine which ye have learned; and avoid them. For they that are such serve not our Lord Jesus Christ . . ." (Rom. 16:17–18).

We ought to mind our tongues, never permitting them to speak hasty, cruel, unkind, or wicked words. We should close our ears to wicked speeches, songs, or words. To do this we must mind our hearts so that the love for sin does not dwell in them. When we permit Jesus to be enthroned in our hearts and refuse to give place to the devil, we shall be victorious over criticism, either as its object or its instrument.

In the midst of criticism it may be helpful to remember what Edward Everett Hale, the American clergyman and author, said to an indignant Bostonian who was angered about some personal criticism in Hale's newspaper. "Now calm yourself," Hale said to him. "Not half the people in this city take that paper, not half of those who take it read it, not half of those who read it saw that particular item, not half of those who read that statement believed it, and not half of those who believed are of any consequence."

"Speak not evil of another, brethren. He that speaketh evil of his brother, and judgeth his brother, speaketh evil of the law, and judgeth the law: but if thou judge the law, thou art not a doer of the law, but a judge" (James 4:11).

A Christian worker was asked by a friend to answer a criticism because it seemed to be doing great harm to the cause for which he had sacrificed for many years. After thinking about the request that would involve writing a defense for a Christian work that needed no defense, he told his friend he would not reply to what was said against him and the work he was doing for the Lord. His decision was based on two simple facts: his friends did not need his defense and his enemies would not believe him anyway.

"If the world hate you, ye know that it hated me before it hated you. If ye were of the world, the world would love his own: but because ye are not of the world, but I have chosen you out of the world, therefore the world hateth you" (John 15:18–19). "Woe unto you, when all men shall speak well of you! for so did their fathers to the false prophets" (Luke 6:26).

When criticism comes, consider the source and the motive. If it is from someone who loves you and desires your best, take it and profit therefrom. If you do wrong and a brother seeks to restore you, you do well to respond. Criticism given in a spirit of love, with a genuine desire to help one walk in obedience to God, should be received with gratitude. On the other hand, if the criticism comes from a sour saint or a godless sinner and the criticism is not valid, forget it. Just keep going on for God.

For further study: Luke 6:37–42; John 7:24; Rom. 2:1–4; 14:1–15; I Cor. 13:1, 4–6; Gal. 6:1–4.

MONOTONY

Monotony can be dangerous. If there is a persistent sameness or want of variety in life, one may be open to temptation unknown to those who are actively involved in many pursuits. C. S. Lewis said, "The long, dull, monotonous years of middle-aged prosperity or middle-aged adversity are excellent campaigning weather for the devil." This need not be true, but unfortunately it sometimes is. The devil can use daily sameness to discourage and destroy motivation to pursue new and greater goals.

Desperate actions occasionally result when individuals are locked into the same unexciting details of life as they experience it. In his *Fireside Travels,* James Russell Lowell wrote, "There is nothing so desperately monotonous as the sea, and I no longer wonder at the cruelty of pirates."

On the other hand, if everyone of us would seek to eliminate the ordinary and go looking for change, variety, and excitement, little or nothing would ever be finished. What has seemed monotonous to some has brought success beyond what one would expect to others. Thomas Edison said, "I never did anything worth doing by accident, nor did any of my inventions come by accident." He once told a friend that fifty-eight recent experiments had come to nothing. "How awful!" consoled the friend. "It must be terribly discouraging to have so many failures." "Oh, they were not failures," responded Edison cheerfully. "Now I know fifty-eight ways that won't work."

In these days when some in the women's liberation movement look at the woman's place in the home, they are complaining that their roles as wives and mothers leave no time or opportunity for so-called creative tasks. A woman's place in the home need not be one of monotony. In answer to this charge someone asked, "What could be more creative than creating new life and a happy home?"

If you are becoming tired of your worka-day world, listen to the good advice of Theodore Roosevelt, a man of action all his life. He said, "No man needs sympathy because he has to work. Far and away the best prize that life offers is the chance to work hard at work worth doing."

Distasteful monotony will disappear when one considers what God does for him every day. "Blessed be the Lord, who daily loadeth us with benefits, even the God of our salvation" (Ps. 68:19). The Amplified Bible says it like this: "Blessed be the Lord, Who bears our burdens, and carries us day by day, even the God Who is our salvation." Who can complain about monotony when he knows the God who loads him with blessings and carries him along day by day? God provides new roads for us to travel every day; however, we may think we are covering the same territory if we are without a vision of new scenery.

Each day God has something new and different for His children who *look* for it. "It is of the Lord's mercies that we are not consumed, because his compassions fail not. They are new every morning: great is thy faithfulness" (Lam. 3:22–23). The psalmist wrote, ". . . His favor is for a lifetime . . . but . . . joy comes in the morning" (Ps. 30:5, NASB). When we walk with the Lord, life does not have an unbearable sameness. It possesses the quality of excitement as He unfolds new lessons and blessings.

The cure for monotony, then, is a personal experience with the Savior who does not change but leads His people into pathways that are new and challenging to them. When you trust and obey, monotony will flee away.

For further study: Ps. 1:1–3; 25:4, 5; 119:97, 105; Prov. 4:18; Isa. 40:31; I Cor. 4:16; Eph. 6:10, 11, 13.